**ISBN  0 9511458 1 9  Heritage Trams  (card cover)**

First published in Great Britain 1991
by **TRAMBOOKS**
48 Dorrington Road, Cheadle Heath, Stockport, SK3 OPZ
and printed by The Commercial Centre Ltd
Clowes Street, Hollinwood, Oldham

By the same author:
**Tramcar Treasury**
**Transport Treasures of Trafford Park**
**On the Trams**

*ACKNOWLEDGMENTS*
*The publishers are grateful to all those who have assisted with*
*providing information and photographs for this book, especially the*
*officials of the museums and tramway systems who have dealt with our*
*enquiries. Those private individuals who have been particularly helpful*
*include Les Brunton (Newcastle), Colin Cartwright (Walsall), Richard*
*Delahoy (Southend), Frank Dix (London), Philip Groves (Nottingham),*
*David Hanson (Manchester), Bob Hill (Altrincham), Raymond Hughes*
*(Altrincham), Rob Jones (Wallasey), Hugh McAuley (Glasgow), Tim*
*Major (Lowestoft), Stuart Rivers (Llandudno), Jim Shearer (Blackpool),*
*Ron Smith (Cardiff), Tony Stevenson (Lytham), Colin Stringer*
*(Stalybridge), Ray Tabraham (Hassocks), Richard Wall (Walsall),*
*Stanley Webb (Walsall).*

*Front cover:* Sheffield No 264 at Beamish, the North of England Open
Air Museum; the display of trams at the Glasgow Museum of Transport,
and London No 1858 on duty at the East Anglia Transport Museum,
Lowestoft.

*Frontispiece:* London tramcar No 1858 emerges from the woodland
track at the East Anglia Transport Museum

Metropolitan Electric Tramways No 331 stops to pick up passengers at
the National Tramway Museum at Crich in Derbyshire, one of the
attractions described in this guide. When this car was introduced on
London streets it heralded a new concept in tramcar travel - and still
looks modern today. It was the only tram with centre entrance in
London - and ran on the Whetstone-Cricklewood service. Its high
capacity required two conductors at busy periods. (Colin Stringer)

# HERITAGE TRAMS

## by Dennis Gill

**BEAMISH**

### NORTH OF ENGLAND OPEN AIR MUSEUM

One of the most evocative of Britain's heritage tramways is found in County Durham at Beamish, the North of England Open Air Museum, where visitors can take a trip into the living past. Beautiful restored trams, with drivers and conductors in period costume, take visitors from the museum entrance to a reconstructed old town of yesteryear.

Set in 300 acres of woodland and rolling countryside, the museum is a unique example of what life in the North of England was really like in the early years of the century. It includes a farm, colliery, mining village, and railway station as well as an old Co-op store, bandstand and

*Sheffield balcony tram No 264 sets off from Beamish Museum's recreated town. On the right is the reconstructed co-operative store from Annfield Plain - a big favourite with visitors.*

fairground. There is also a replica of a 1914 open-top bus on which visitors can ride, and a trolleybus from Newcastle. The railway

exhibits include a working replica of the famous locomotive built by George Stephenson in 1825. Beamish was the first open-air museum

to be established in Britain, and was deservedly Museum of the Year in 1986, and European Museum of the Year in 1987.

*Enjoying fresh air at the open air museum - visitors to Beamish take a nostalgic trip to the past.*

*Pause between trips. Gateshead 10 takes a break outside the depot at Beamish. (Colin Stringer)*

Beamish, The North of England
Open Air Museum
Beamish, Co. Durham, DH9 ORG
**Tel:** 0207 231811
**Opening times:** Easter-Oct, daily
10am-6pm; Nov-Easter, Tues-
Sun, 10am-5pm. Check for
Christmas opening times.
**Admission:** Charge payable
**Amenities:** *Free tram rides *Car
parking *Shop *Tea room
**Location:** Near Stanley. Follow
signs on A1(M), A693 or A68
**Track:** 1 mile (opened 1973)
**Gauge:** standard

**Tramcars:**

BEAMISH 196
Four-wheel Ex-Oporto
single-decker

BLACKPOOL 31
Four-wheel open-topper built by
Midland Railway Carriage and
Wagon 1901 (On loan from
Blackpool Corporation)

GATESHEAD 10
Enclosed 8-wheel single-decker
built by Gateshead & District
Tramways 1925 (On loan from
Science Museum, London)

SHEFFIELD 264
Four-wheel balcony car built by
United Electric Car 1927  (On
loan from Science Museum)

SHEFFIELD 513
Enclosed 4-wheel double-decker
built by Chas Roberts 1952  (On
loan from Castle Museum, York)

**To be restored:**

NEWCASTLE 114
Four-wheel unvestibuled balcony
car built by Hurst Nelson 1901

SUNDERLAND 16
Enclosed 4-wheel double-decker
built by Dick, Kerr 1900

*Living history. Tram crews at Beamish dress in period costume to give an authentic impression of travel in the early years of the century. This driver is at the controls of Blackpool open-top tramcar No 31, which arrived at the museum in 1984 and was restored to its present condition in 1988. The trams at Beamish link most of the museum's attractions, starting at the visitor centre and terminating in the reconstructed market town.*

*Douglas horse tram No 46 on view at the Woodside Visitors' centre in Birkenhead. The tram was built in Birkenhead, the first town in the British Isles to have trams and manufacture them. The town plans to commemorate this fact by building a dockside heritage tramway which will terminate near the rejuvenated Mersey ferry building, where the centre is now housed. Before being shipped to Birkenhead, the horse tram served as a playground attraction at Douglas.*

# BELFAST

## BELFAST TRANSPORT MUSEUM

Tramcars of three gauges are exhibited at the Belfast Transport Museum, established by Belfast Museum and Art Galleries in the late 1950's. There are examples of standard gauge, wide gauge (5ft 3in) and narrow gauge (3ft). The standard gauge vehicles comprise electric and horse-drawn trams from Belfast. The wide gauge exhibits are an electric car from the scenic Hill of Howth tourist line near Dublin and a horse car that ran from 1883 to 1957 at Fintona, County Tyrone. The narrow gauge is represented by a steam tram from Portstewart and by electric single-deck cars from the Bessbrook and Newry line and the Giant's Causeway tramway.

The collection was taken over by the Ulster Folk Museum in 1967 and will eventually be transferred to Cultra in County Down.

Belfast Transport Museum
Witham Street, Belfast
**Tel:** 0232 451519
**Opening times:** Daily (except Sundays), 10am-5pm
**Admission:** Charge payable
**Amenities:** *Shop
**Location:** Two miles east of city centre, off Newtownards Road, close to Glentoran football ground
**Tramcars:**
BELFAST 357
Enclosed 4-wheel double-decker built by Brush 1929
BELFAST 249
Four-wheel open-topper converted from horse tram by Belfast CT 1905

BELFAST STREET TRAMWAYS 118
Double-deck horse tram built by Belfast Street Tramways 1885
BESSBROOK & NEWRY 2
Enclosed 8-wheel single-decker built by Mather & Platt 1885
FINTONA 381
Double-deck horse tram built by Metropolitan Carriage 1883
GIANT'S CAUSEWAY 5
Single-deck toastrack trailer built by Metropolitan Carriage 1883
GIANT'S CAUSEWAY 2
Single-deck saloon trailer built by Metropolitan Carriage 1883 (displayed at Cultra)
HILL OF HOWTH 4
Eight-wheel open-topper built by Milnes 1901
PORTSTEWART 2
Steam tram locomotive built by Kitson 1883

# BIRKENHEAD

## WOODSIDE VISITOR CENTRE

Department of Leisure Services and Tourism, Westminster House, Hamilton Street, Birkenhead, Wirral L41 5FN

**Tel:** 051-647 2366

**Opening times:** Daily
**Admission:** Free

**Amenities:** *Shop *Cafe
**Location:** Woodside Ferry
**Tramcar exhibit:**

DOUGLAS 46
Roofed crossbench horse car built by Milnes Voss 1909 (On loan from Douglas Corporation)

*Belfast horse tram No 118 - one of the exhibits at Belfast Transport Museum - on parade in the sixties. (Belfast Newsletter)*

*Birmingham balcony car No 395 - on show at the Birmingham Museum of Science and Industry. The car is the sole completely-intact survivor of the city's fleet of 843 cars, which were well maintained and had excellent riding qualities, fast acceleration and comfortable upholstered seating. A hundred cars like this were built in 1911-12 and they gave many years' faithful service. No 395 entered the museum in 1953, after serving for a while as a works shunter following its withdrawal from passenger service in November 1950. (Birmingham Museum of Science and Industry)*

*Frankfurt 210 lines up with preserved buses at the Birmingham and Midland Museum of Transport (EN Pounder)*

# BIRMINGHAM

## BIRMINGHAM AND MIDLAND MUSEUM OF TRANSPORT

This museum is being developed as a regional road transport heritage centre. Its exhibits include a tramcar imported from Frankfurt, and there are plans to build an operating tramway.

Birmingham and Midland Museum of Transport

Chapel Lane, Wythall, Birmingham B47 6JX

**Tel:** Info from 0543 253941

**Opening times:** Easter-Nov, Sat and Sun; event days on the first Sunday of every month and bank holiday Sun and Mon, 11am-5pm

**Admission:** Charge payable

**Amenities:** *Shop *Car Parking * Refreshments on event days

**Location:** Off A435 Birmingham to Evesham Road

**Tramcar:**

FRANKFURT 210
Four-axle single-ended single-decker built by Duwag 1955

## BIRMINGHAM MUSEUM OF SCIENCE AND INDUSTRY

There are a number of fascinating transport halls in the Birmingham Museum of Science and Industry - and the smallest, the Tramhouse, contains Birmingham Corporation 3ft 6in-gauge electric car No 395. The tram, which was

*Resplendent in a pre-1933 livery, Blackpool double-deck tram No 701 makes ready for another trip along Blackpool promenade. (John Clarkson)*

presented by the Birmingham Common Good Trust in 1953, is displayed with other tramway memorabilia, providing a fascinating contrast to the locomotives and various vehicles in the other halls.

Birmingham Museum of Science and Industry

Newhall Street, Birmingham, West Midlands B3 1RZ
**Tel:** 021-236 1022

**Opening times:** Daily (except Christmas and 1 Jan) 9.30am-5pm (Sun 2-5pm)

**Admission:** *Free

**Amenities:** *Shop *Multi-storey car park nearby

**Location:** Close to city centre alongside Birmingham Canal

**Exhibits:**

BIRMINGHAM 395
Four-wheel balcony car built by United Electric Car 1912

EMB maximum traction bogie and a controller

Scale models of Birmingham Corporation enclosed electric tramcar No 777 and a City of Birmingham steam tram engine and trailer

## BLACKPOOL

### BLACKPOOL COASTAL TRAMWAY

Blackpool's tramway system is older than the tower and almost as famous. Opened in 1885, it was the first electric tramway in Britain and has outlived all the others that followed in its wake. The trams, which celebrated a century of continuous operation in 1985, give holidaymakers a sea front ride

from one end of the resort to the other, with some continuing further to Fleetwood - a distance of 11 miles. The rolling stock varies from very modern 8-wheel vehicles built in recent years to much older cars loaned as tourist attractions by various museums (including the National Tramway Museum) or by groups of enthusiasts. There are also a number of illuminated cars which glide up and down the promenade ablaze with colour during the autumn 'Lights' period.

Blackpool Transport Services

Rigby Road, Blackpool, Lancs FY1 5DD

**Tel:** 0253 23931

**Opening times:** Trams operate daily from about 6am to midnight (including Christmas Day)

**Charges:** Fares payable on cars. An all-day ticket giving unlimited travel on trams and buses is available from drivers and conductors.

**Route:** 11.5 miles, Blackpool (Starr Gate) to Fleetwood Ferry

**Gauge:** standard

**Rolling stock:**

More than 70 double-deck and single-deck cars:

Double-deckers: Nos 700-704, 706, 707-713, 715-724, 726, 761-762, all built by English Electric 1934 (Nos 761 and 762 rebuilt by Blackpool 1982, and 706 converted to open top by Blackpool 1985)

Tower and trams are synonymous with Blackpool. The trams started running on the promenade in 1885, and the Tower was opened in 1894. Both the cars pictured here were built in the thirties, as part of a big modernisation programme. and because of their rounded appearance are nicknamed 'Balloons.' Seating 94, they have proved invaluable in carrying the thousands of holidaymakers who visit the resort each year.

Bolton tram No. 66 has run in service at Blackpool for the past decade. It was painstakingly reconstructed by Bolton tram lovers over a period of 18 years and is a classic example of tramcar restoration. Many of the holidaymakers who ride on it and admire its high standard of finish find it hard to believe that after its withdrawal from service in 1946 it served as a chicken coop for many years. It is shown here on a special tour. (Colin Stringer)

*One of Blackpool's modern Centenary cars - a single decker with bus-like features. It has a front entrance and centre exit and was built by East Lancashire Coachbuilders of Blackburn, who also built the bodywork for Blackpool's Atlantean buses. It is called a 'Centenary' car because it was built for the hundredth anniversary of Blackpool's tramway, celebrated in 1985. A total of eight Centenary cars have been placed in service. (Blackpool Transport Services Ltd)*

Enclosed single deckers: Nos 5, 8, 10, 11 (built by English Electric 1934-5 and rebuilt by Blackpool 1972-6); 621-3, 625-7, 630-4, 636-7 (built by Brush 1937); 641-8 (built by East Lancs Coachbuilders 1984-8); 660 (built by Charles Roberts 1953); 678-80 (built 1935 and rebuilt 1960-1 by English Electric)

Open single-deckers: Nos 600 (on loan to Heaton Park), 602, 604-7 (built by Blackpool 1934)

Trailer sets: Nos 671/681, 672/682, 673/683, 674/684, 675/685, 676/686, 677/687 (towing cars built 1935 and rebuilt 1963 by English Electric; trailer cars built by Metropolitan Cammell-Weymann 1960)

Crossbench single-decker: No 619 (built by Bolton Trams 1987)

Illuminated cars: Nos 732-6 (built by Blackpool 1960-5)

**Cars on loan:**

BLACKPOOL AND FLEETWOOD 40
Enclosed 8-wheel single-decker built by United Electric Car 1914 (On loan from National Tramway Museum)

BOLTON 66
Unvestibuled 8-wheel double-decker built by the Electric Railway and Tramway Carriage in 1901 and rebuilt by Bolton Trams 1980

# BOURNEMOUTH

## BOURNEMOUTH HERITAGE TRANSPORT CENTRE

Bournemouth's heritage transport collection of trams, trolleybuses and buses is housed in a busy working transport depot. Consequently visitors can only view the collection during the times specified. Prize exhibit among the tramcars is the narrow-gauge Bournemouth No. 85, which after 22 years' service in the resort ran for a further 20 years between Llandudno and Colwyn Bay. It is hoped this car, and other old tram bodies which have been acquired, will eventually run on a working tramway. The collection is unusual in having a bus which has been converted into a mobile museum, containing many parts recovered from Bournemouth No 89.

Bournemouth Heritage Transport Centre

Yellow Buses Depot, Mallard Road, Bournemouth

**Tel:** 0202 485837

**Opening times:** Sat and Sun 10.30am-5.30pm. Also in summer Tue and Fri evenings 7-9.00pm and Wed 10.30am-5.30pm

**Admission:** Charge payable
**Amenities:** *Souvenirs sold in tram shop

**Location:** Near Hampshire Shopping Centre on Castle Lane, Charminster (A3060)

**Tramcars:**

BOURNEMOUTH 85
Eight-wheel open-topper built by United Electric Car 1914 (On

loan from Science Museum, London)

**Tramcar bodies awaiting restoration:**

BOURNEMOUTH 13
Eight-wheel open-topper built by Milnes 1902 (In store)

BOURNEMOUTH 31 and 42
Four-wheel open-toppers built by Milnes 1902 (In store)

BOURNEMOUTH 53
Eight-wheel open-topper built by Milnes 1904 (In store)

BOURNEMOUTH 72
Eight-wheel open-topper built by Brush 1906 (In store)

BOURNEMOUTH 101
Eight-wheel open-topper built by Brush 1906

POOLE 6
Four-wheel open-topper built by Dick, Kerr 1901

# BRADFORD

## BRADFORD INDUSTRIAL MUSEUM

Although the Bradford Industrial Museum specialises in worsted textile machinery it has other attractions, including horses at work, a living display of working shire horses and their vehicles, and transport galleries housing a Bradford tram and trolleybus and Bradford-built Jowett cars. The tram, the last to run in Bradford, served for a number of years as a scoreboard at Odsal stadium before being rescued by two Bradford tramway enthusiasts and restored to pristine condition in 1958. The museum plans to operate a working tramway line.

Bradford Industrial Museum
Moorside Mills, Moorside Road, Bradford BD2 3HP

**Tel:** 0274 631756

**Opening times:** Tues-Sun, 10am-5pm (Closed Christmas and Good Friday, but open Bank Holiday Monday)

**Admission:** Free

**Amenities:** *Shop *Cafe *Car parking

**Location:** Signposted from Bradford Ring Road and Harrogate Road

**Tramcar:**

BRADFORD 104
Four-wheel balcony car built by Bradford CT 1925

Also tramway artefacts including stop signs, etc. and model trams

## WEST YORKSHIRE TRANSPORT MUSEUM

Continental single-deckers form the basis of the tramway collection at the West Yorkshire Transport Museum in Bradford. They have been acquired for eventual operation on a museum tramway that will be laid in the Spen Valley between Low Moor and Heckmondwike. The collection, which also includes a Blackpool tram, is at present housed in the former Bradford Corporation bus garage in Ludlam Street.

*Bradford balcony car No. 104 - the first tram in Britain to be resurrected and restored for preservation - gives rides at Thornbury bus depot in Bradford. It is now on display in Bradford Industrial Museum.*

The building has a distinctive Egyptian-style frontage and a colourful mural depicting a tram and trolleybus. The museum also plans to restore a number of tram bodies from various Yorkshire towns and cities.

West Yorkshire Transport Museum

Ludlam Street Depot, Mill Lane, off Manchester Road, Bradford BD5 0HG

**Tel:** 0274 736006

**Opening times:** Every Sunday, 11am-5pm

**Admission:** Charge payable

**Amenities:** *Shop *Cafe *Car parking

**Location:** On Manchester Road (A641), a mile from city centre

**Tramcars:**

BLACKPOOL 663
Enclosed 8-wheel 'Coronation' single-decker built by Charles Roberts 1953

BUDAPEST 2576/2577
Coupled 8-wheel enclosed single-deckers built by Ganz 1904

ROTTERDAM 109/115
Enclosed 8-wheel single-decker and trailer built by Allan 1950

Bradford No. 104 on display at the Bradford Industrial Museum. Brilliantly illuminated and decorated with colourful bunting, it was the last tram to run in Bradford in 1950, and afterwards served in the unusual role of scorebox at Odsal Stadium. Rescued in 1953, it was restored to its original condition over a period of five years. A walkway at the side of the car enables visitors to peer into the lower saloon.

Bournemouth tramcar No. 85, which can be seen in Bournemouth's heritage transport centre. This car, which was very popular with holidaymakers, gave faithful service on both the Bournemouth and Llandudno and Colwyn Bay systems. It was one of the last open-toppers to operate in this country. After being withdrawn from service in 1956, it joined the Museum of British Transport at Clapham in London, moving back to Bournemouth in 1974.

Bradford's electric tramway system was one of the earliest in Britain, and it had the biggest fleet of 4ft gauge trams. The different types of car are represented by these handsome models on display at the Bradford Industrial Museum. They were made by Bradford tramway historian Frank Hartley and include (right) two ex-Mid Yorkshire cars which were absorbed in the Bradford fleet in 1904.

This Budapest car and trailer is one of the attractions in the West Yorkshire Transport Museum at Ludlam Street, Bradford, which plans to run electric trams in the Spen Valley between Low Moor and Heckmondwike. The car was shipped over to Bradford in 1985, after running for many years on the streets of Hungary's capital.

*Cardiff Tramways horse car No. 21 - once a tea bar, now a transport exhibit at the Welsh Industrial and Maritime Museum in Cardiff. (Welsh Industrial and Maritime Museum)*

Volk's Electric Railway,
Madeira Drive, Brighton

**Tel:** 0273 681061

**Opening times:** Apr-Sep, daily, 11am-6pm

**Charges:** Fares payable

**Location:** On sea front

**Track:** 1.25 miles

**Gauge:** 2ft 9in

**Rolling stock:**

Nos 1-9 Four crossbench and five semi-open 4-wheel single deckers, built 1890-1927

## BROADSTAIRS KENT

### CRAMPTON TOWER MUSEUM

High Street, Broadstairs, Kent

**Tel:** 0843 64446

**Opening times:** Good Fri-Oct, Mon, Tues, Thurs, Fri and Bank Holiday Sundays, 2.30-5pm

**Admission:** Charge payable

**Amenities:** *Shop

**Location:** Adjacent to Station

**Tramway exhibits:**

Memorabilia of Isle of Thanet tramway, including tram seats

## CARDIFF

### HEATH PARK TRAMWAY

A pioneer of parkland miniature tramways is the 18-inch gauge passenger-carrying line in Cardiff's

ROTTERDAM 408
Enclosed 8-wheel single-decker built by Allan 1929
Also a Brussels snowbroom car
**Bodies to be restored include:**

BRADFORD 54 (standard balcony)

LEEDS 324 (balcony)

HALIFAX 82 (balcony)

HUDDERSFIELD 2 (short-roof open-topper)

DEWSBURY AND OSSETT (open-topper)

YORKSHIRE WOOLLEN 57

## BRIGHTON

### VOLK'S ELECTRIC RAILWAY

The first electric railway to open in Britain is still operating at Brighton. The cars which run on the line are more like trams than trains, and provide a valuable service on Brighton's sea front, from Palace Pier to the Brighton

Marina Village  The railway opened on 4 August 1883 and was built by the man after whom it is named - Magnus Volk, the inventive and innovative son of a German clockmaker.  Cars built for the line in the 1890's are still in service, collecting their current from a third rail.  The fleet also includes two cars which ran on the Southend-on-Sea pier railway from 1890 until 1949.

Heath Park. In the form of a horse shoe, the line is one of Heath Park's most popular weekend attractions. It was built by members of the Whitchurch and District Model Engineering Society and boasts two handsome cars - both designed by the Society's octogenarian president, Felix Cunuder, formerly chief engineer of Cardiff Corporation Transport. The tramway is operated by members on certain Sundays and Bank Holiday weekends, but can be viewed on non-running days by appointment.

Heath Park Tramway

Heath Park, Cardiff

**Tel:** 0222 752881 (Mr F Cunuder)

**Opening times:** Bank Holidays and certain Sundays, 2-5.30pm

**Charges:** *Fares payable

**Amenities:** *Snack bar *Car parking

**Location:** Off King George Vth Drive East

**Track length:** 350 yds (Opened 1987)

**Gauge:** 18-inch

**Rolling stock:**

No 1 Crossbench 4-wheel single-decker (1973)

No 2 Modern 8-wheel semi-closed single-decker (1976)

Both cars built by Whitchurch and District Model Engineering Society

## WELSH INDUSTRIAL AND MARITIME MUSEUM

A horse tram which once served as a dockland tea bar run by the Cardiff Ladies Temperance Movement is preserved at the Welsh Industrial and Maritime Museum in Cardiff. It was acquired by the museum in 1980 and is fully restored to its original condition and livery. The restoration work was done as a job-creation project to teach joinery to young people and was completed in 1982. The museum, which also includes a railway exhibition housed in the nearby Bute Station, plans to construct an operating tramway sometime in the future.

Welsh Industrial and Maritime Museum

Bute Street, Cardiff CF1 6AN

**Tel:** 0222 481919

**Opening times:** Tues-Sat, 10am-5pm; Sun 2.30-5pm (closed Christmas and New Year, Good Friday and May Day)

**Admission:** *Free

**Amenities:** *Shop *Car parking

**Location:** Butetown dock area of Cardiff

**Tramcar:**

CARDIFF TRAMWAYS CO. 21 Double-deck horse car built by Falcon 1885

*More than a century old and still going strong - the Volk's Electric Railway in Brighton. (Philip Groves)*

## COATBRIDGE

### SUMMERLEE HERITAGE MUSEUM

Scotland's one and only heritage tramway is to be found at Coatbridge, near Glasgow. Opened as recently as 1988, it is also Britain's newest heritage tramway, and the only one in Britain operated entirely by foreign cars - from Brussels and Graz. The line is one of the main attractions at the museum, which recreates the sights and sounds of 200 years of Scottish industry. The museum is on the site of the old Summerlee ironworks and inside the main industrial hall an old tram saloon is used to display local historical tramway photographs. Summerlee Museum is restoring an old Lanarkshire tramcar (No 53) to running condition.

Summerlee Heritage Museum

West Canal Street, Coatbridge M15 1QD

**Tel:** 0236 31261

**Opening times:** Daily 10am-5pm

**Admission:** Free

**Amenities:** *Shop *Traditional tea room *Canalside picnic and play area *Car parking

**Location:** close to Coatbridge town centre and Sunnyside and Central stations

*Sharing passenger-carrying duties at the Summerlee Museum at Coatbridge in Scotland are these two trams from Graz (right) and Brussels.*

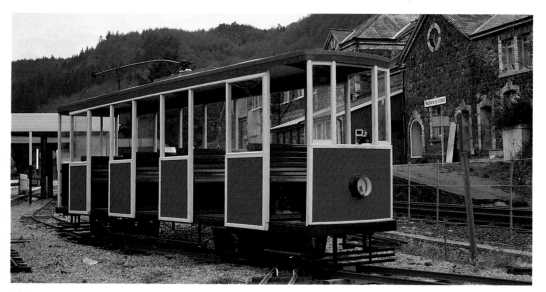

*This miniature passenger-carrying tram has been specially built for the Conwy Valley Railway Museum, and it is hoped to have it running sometime in 1991 (Colin Cartwright)*

**Track length:** 500m (opened 1988 and extended 1991)

**Gauge:** 1435m

**Tramcars:**

BRUSSELS 9062
Enclosed 4-wheel single decker built 1960

GRAZ 225
Enclosed 4-wheel single-decker built 1949

OPORTO 150
Enclosed 4-wheel single-decker built 1912

**Undergoing restoration:**

LANARKSHIRE 53
Four-wheel open-topper built by United Electric Car 1909

# CONWY VALLEY SNOWDONIA

## CONWY VALLEY RAILWAY MUSEUM

Britain's newest miniature tramway is due to open in 1991 at Betws-y-Coed in North Wales. (Check whether running before visiting).

It has been constructed at the Conwy Valley Railway Museum, which already boasts a passenger-carrying miniature railway and some superb model railway layouts. A new tramcar has been purpose-built for the line by a Birmingham engineering firm. It is fitted with controls formerly used on an overhead crane and has seats for 14 adults. The tramway

*Visitors to Cardiff's Heath Park can take pleasure trips on this miniature tram, driven here by the man who designed it - octogenarian Felix Cunuder, former chief engineer of Cardiff City Tramways. It is 12ft long, seats eight, and bears the legend 'Cardiff City Tramways' and the city's coat-of-arms. Its sister tram is a bogie car 20ft long, seating 20. Both cars, and the 18-inch tramway they run on, were built with the help of the Whitchurch and District Model Engineering Society. The line has been in operation, delighting both young and old, since 1987. Previously the Society ran its cars at its former headquarters in Highfield Road. (Ron Smith)*

runs alongside the BR main line and into a wood.

Conwy Valley Railway Museum and Leisure Centre

The Old Goods Yard, Betws-y-Coed, Gwynedd, North Wales LL24 OAL

**Tel:** 0690 710568

**Opening times:** Easter-Oct, daily, 10.30am-5.30pm

**Admission:** Free, but fares will be charged for tram rides

**Amenities:** *Shop *Cafe *Car parking

**Location:** Next to Betws-y-Coed BR goods station. Signposted from A5

**Track length:** Half a mile

**Gauge:** 15-inch

**Rolling stock:**

One crossbench 8-wheel single-decker (with disc brakes) built by TMA Engineering

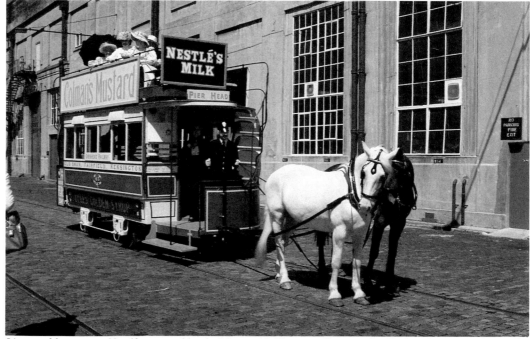

*Liverpool horse tram No. 43, restored by the Merseyside Tramway Preservation Society, is now on view at the National Tramway Museum. (Merseyside Tramway Preservation Society)*

## CRICH DERBYSHIRE

### NATIONAL TRAMWAY MUSEUM

The National Tramway Museum is a Mecca for tram lovers of all ages. It is a living museum where the joy of riding on tramcars of many different shapes, sizes and colours can be experienced to the full. Here, in the heart of Derbyshire, on a hill overlooking the beautiful Derwent valley, a tramway more than a mile long has been constructed largely by voluntary labour, and more than 40 tramcars collected together.

The historic collection includes horse, steam and electric cars from all parts of the British Isles, dating from 1873 to 1952. There are also cars from America, Czechoslovakia, Portugal and South Africa. At least two of the electric cars will be running on any one day. They take visitors on a two-mile round trip down a period tramway street, through a wood and along a hillside giving breathtaking views. The street features a Victorian bridge, band stand, decorative railings, gaslamps, and other items of street furniture acquired from many parts of the country. The museum also has a large exhibition hall (equipped with traverser) and a video theatre, library and archive, and mining display. Special event days are held on certain weekends, including Santa Specials in December.

National Tramway Museum Crich, near Matlock, Derbyshire DE4 5DP

**Tel:** 0773 852565

**Opening times:** Easter-Oct, Sat-Thurs (daily in August) 10am-5.30pm (6.30pm on Sat, Sun and Bank Holidays); also certain Fridays. Santa Specials on December weekends

**Admission:** Charge payable

**Amenities:** *Unlimited tram rides *Shops (souvenirs, books and models) *Cafe *Picnic ground and play area

**Location:** Off B5035, 15 miles north of Derby. Only 8 miles from junction 28 on M1. Follow signs on A6 and A38

**Track length:** 1 mile (opened 1963)

**Gauge:** standard

**Tramcars on display:**

BLACKPOOL 4
Four-wheel single-deck conduit car built by Lancaster Carriage 1884

BLACKPOOL 40
Eight-wheel balcony car built by Blackpool CT 1926

BLACKPOOL 49
Standard 8-wheel double-decker built by Blackpool CT 1926

BLACKPOOL 59
Eight-wheel 4-staircase 'Dreadnought' open-topper built by Midland Railway Carriage and Wagon 1902

BLACKPOOL 166
Toastrack 8-wheel single-decker built by Blackpool CT 1927

BLACKPOOL 167
Enclosed 8-wheel single-decker built by English Electric 1928

BLACKPOOL & FLEETWOOD 2
Crossbench 8-wheel single-decker built by Milnes 1898

BLACKPOOL & FLEETWOOD 40
Enclosed 8-wheel single-decker built by United Electric Car 1914 (On loan to Blackpool Transport)

CHESTERFIELD 8
Single-deck horse tram built by Milnes 1899 (On loan from Science Museum, London)

DERBY 1
Four-wheel open-topper built by Brush 1904

DUNDEE & DISTRICT 21
Eight-wheel double-deck steam tram trailer built by Milnes 1894

DOUGLAS HEAD MARINE DRIVE 1
Crossbench 4-wheel double-decker built by Brush 1896 (On loan from Science Museum, London)

EDINBURGH 35
Enclosed 4-wheel double-decker built by Edinburgh CT 1948 (On loan from Lothian Council)

GATESHEAD & DISTRICT 5
Enclosed 8-wheel single-decker built by Gateshead 1927

GATESHEAD & DISTRICT 52
Enclosed 4-wheel single-decker built by Milnes 1920

GLASGOW 22
Four-wheel balcony car built by Glasgow CT 1922

GLASGOW 812
Standard 4-wheel double-decker built by Glasgow CT 1900

GLASGOW 1100
Enclosed 8-wheel double-decker built by Hurst Nelson 1928

GLASGOW 1115
Enclosed 8-wheel double-decker built by Hurst Nelson 1929

GLASGOW 1282
Enclosed 8-wheel 'Coronation' double-decker built by Glasgow CT 1940

GLASGOW 1297
Enclosed 8-wheel 'Cunarder' double-decker built by Glasgow CT 1948

GRIMSBY & IMMINGHAM 14
Enclosed 8-wheel single-decker built by Great Central Railway 1915

HILL OF HOWTH 10
Eight-wheel open-topper built by Milnes 1902

HULL 132
Enclosed 4-wheel double-decker built by Hull CT 1909 (On loan to Hull Museum of Transport)

JOHANNESBURG 60
Unvestibuled 4-wheel balcony car built by United Electric Car 1902

LCC 106
Four-wheel open-topper built by Electric Railway and Tramway Carriage 1903

LEEDS 180
Enclosed 4-wheel double-decker built by Brush 1931

LEEDS 399
Unvestibuled 4-wheel double-decker built by Leeds CT 1926

LEEDS 600
Centre-entrance 8-wheel single-decker built by Brush 1930

*Southampton 45 approaches the Bowes-Lyon bridge at the National Tramway Museum. This tram was the first to be preserved by the enthusiasts who founded the museum.*

*Making a two-mile round trip on the Crich tramway, Glasgow No. 22, packed with passengers, pauses at a scenic spot en route. Glasgow trams had different-coloured upper-deck panels to distinguish which route they ran on; the white cars, like this one, ran to the University or Hampden Park.*

**LEEDS 602**
'Coronation' 8-wheel single-decker built by Charles Roe 1953

**LEICESTER 76**
Unvestibuled 4-wheel balcony car built by Electric Railway and Tramway Carriage 1904

**LIVERPOOL 43**
Double-deck horse tram built by Liverpool Tramway Company 1879 (On loan from Merseyside Tramway Preservation Society)

**LIVERPOOL 869**
'Green Goddess' 8-wheel double-decker built by Liverpool CPT 1936

**LONDON TRANSPORT 1**
Enclosed 8-wheel double-decker built by LCC 1932

**MANCHESTER 765**
'California' type 8-wheel single-decker built by Hurst Nelson 1901 (On loan to Heaton Park tramway, Manchester)

**METROPOLITAN ELECTRIC 331**
Centre-entrance 8-wheel 'Feltham' double-decker built by Union Construction 1929

**NEWCASTLE 102**
Eight-wheel open-topper built by Hurst Nelson 1901

**NEW SOUTH WALES 2**
Steam tram locomotive built by Beyer Peacock 1885

**NEW YORK 674**
Enclosed 8-wheel single-decker built by Third Avenue Transit 1939

**OPORTO 9**
Single-deck horse car built by Starbuck 1873

**PAISLEY DISTRICT 68**
Four-wheel open-topper built by Hurst Nelson 1919

*Top-notch restoration for an eye-catching London tram - Metropolitan Electric Tramways No. 331 on duty at the National Tramway Museum. This car was one of the experimental modern double-deck Feltham-type trams built for the MET in 1930, with comfortable seating for 66 passengers, centre entrance and raised cab. It was sold in 1937 to Sunderland, where it ran, as No. 100, until 1954. In 1990, sporting a bright blue and white British Steel livery, it carried thousands of passengers at the Gateshead Garden Festival.*

*Gleaming in the Crich sunshine is newly-restored Leeds No. 399 - one of the cars to be given a thorough overhaul in the National Tramway Museum workshops. It was the first double-deck tram to arrive at the museum in 1959, and has been painted in the pre-1939 Leeds livery of chocolate and primrose. In Leeds it worked mainly on the hilly Beeston service, for which purpose it was equipped with air-brakes.*

PRAGUE 180
Enclosed 4-wheel single-decker
built by Ringhoffer 1905

SHEFFIELD 15
Single-deck horse car built by
Starbuck 1874

SHEFFIELD 46
Enclosed 4-wheel single-decker
built by Milnes 1899

SHEFFIELD 74
Four-wheel short-canopy double-
decker built by Dick, Kerr 1900

SHEFFIELD 189
Enclosed 4-wheel double-decker
built by Sheffield CT 1934

SHEFFIELD 264
Enclosed 4-wheel double-decker
built by Sheffield CT 1937

SHEFFIELD 510
Enclosed 4-wheel double-decker
built by Charles Roberts 1950

SOUTHAMPTON 45
Four-wheel open-topper built by
Hurst Nelson 1903

Also six works cars

**Tramcars in store, undergoing
or awaiting restoration:**

BLACKPOOL 298
Eight-wheel single-deck railcoach
built by Brush 1937

CHESTERFIELD 7
Unvestibuled 4-wheel balcony car
built by Brush 1904

LEEDS 345
Enclosed 4-wheel double-decker
built by Hurst Nelson 1921

LONDON 1622
Enclosed 8-wheel double-decker
built by Brush 1912 and being
restored by LCC Tramways Trust
in London

*Douglas horse tram No. 14 arrives at the Manx Museum. (Manx
Museum and National Trust, Douglas)*

# DOUGLAS

## DOUGLAS HORSE
## TRAMWAY

When the Queen visited the
Isle of Man in 1972 she was
conveyed along Douglas
promenade by one of the
resort's famous horse trams.
After alighting from the car
she fed Pearl, the roan mare in
the traces, with sugar lumps.
Other members of the Royal
Family have also taken
trips on the tramway -
recognising the unique
position it occupies on the
world transport scene. Not
only has it been in existence
longer than any other horse
tramway (it opened in 1876)
but also it has the largest fleet
of horse cars.

The horse trams are also the
only ones in the world
operating a regular passenger-
carrying service on a public
highway. They run at a
leisurely six miles an hour,
hauled by home bred horses,
giving a relaxing and
refreshing jaunt round the
sweep of Douglas bay - an
experience in marked contrast
to modern day road traffic.
Part of the horse tram sheds at
Derby Castle are given over to
museum exhibits. These
include a restored cable car,
three historic horse trams (one
of which is fitted out as a
souvenir shop) and a showcase
of relics from the cable trams
and a cut-away of cable track.

Douglas Horse Tramway
Stathallan Crescent, Douglas,
Isle of Man

**Tel:** 0624 675222

**Opening times:** May and Sep,
9am-6pm; Jun-Aug 9am-8.30pm

**Charges:** Fares payable on cars

**Amenities:** *Souvenir shop at
Derby Castle

**Route:** 1.6 miles, along Douglas
Promenade, from Victoria
Steamer Pier to Derby Castle
**Gauge:** 3ft

**Rolling stock:** 18 operational
single-deck horse cars:

Nos 32-37, 43-45 (roofed
crossbench); 21, 38-40, 42
(toastrack); 1, 27-29 (saloons)
built 1890-1909, all by Milnes,
except 1, 42, 45 (Milnes Voss)
and 43, 44 (United Electric Car)

**Tramcar exhibits:**

DOUGLAS 72/73
Crossbench 8-wheel single-deck
cable car, reconstructed 1976
using parts of cable cars 72 and
73 built by Milnes 1896

DOUGLAS 12
Short toastrack horse car built by
Milnes 1888

**DOUGLAS 18**
Open-top horse car (ex-South Shields) built by Midland Railway Carriage and Wagon 1883 and rebuilt 1988. (Used operationally on limited basis)

**DOUGLAS 22**
Single-deck toastrack horse car built by Milnes 1890 and converted to mobile shop

## MANX MUSEUM

Douglas, Isle of Man

**Tel:** 0624 675522

**Opening times:** Mon-Sat, 10am-5pm (except Good Friday, Christmas and Tynwald Day)

**Admission:** Free

**Amenities:** *Shop *Car parking *Access for wheelchairs

**Tramcar exhibit:**

**DOUGLAS 14**
Double-deck horse car (ex-South Shields) built by Midland Railway Carriage and Wagon 1883 (On loan from Science Museum, London)

# DOVER

## DOVER TRANSPORT MUSEUM

Connaught Pumping Station, Connaught Road, Dover, Kent

**Tel:** 0304 204612

**Opening times:** Easter-end of Sep, Fri 2pm-5pm; Sun 11am-5pm (Group visits at other times by prior arrangement)

**Admission:** Charge payable

**Amenities:** *Shop *Refreshments *Car parking

*Dublin No. 253, one of the trams restored in Ireland. (National Transport Museum, Ireland)*

**Exhibits:**
Model tramway layout, 32ft long, with three-quarter-inch scale models of narrow-gauge Dover, Isle of Thanet and Maidstone cars

Working model of Folkestone Leas cliff lift

Photographic display of Dover and Hythe & Sandgate systems

**Undergoing restoration:**

**HASTINGS 43**
Four-wheel open-topper built by Electric Railway and Tramway Carriage 1906

# DUBLIN

## NATIONAL TRANSPORT MUSEUM

Howth Castle, Dublin 13, Ireland

**Tel:** 01 480831/475623/887030

**Opening times:** Easter-Oct, Sat, Sun, Bank Hols 2-5pm; Summer 2-6pm

**Admission:** Charge payable

**Amenities:** *Limited car parking

**Location:** In Castle grounds. Short walk from Howth Station.

**Tramcars:**

Undergoing restoration:

**DUBLIN UNITED**
Directors' car built 1901 (fire damaged)

**DUBLIN UNITED 253**
Enclosed 8-wheel double-decker built by Dublin United 1928

**GIANT'S CAUSEWAY 9**
Single-decker built 1887

**HILL OF HOWTH 9**
Eight-wheel open-topper built by Milnes 1902

**LCC T24**
Four-wheel open-top trailer built by Brush 1917

# DUDLEY

## BLACK COUNTRY MUSEUM

Nearly a million and a half passengers have been carried by Dudley and Stourbridge No 5 since it started running at the Black Country Museum in 1980. For a decade it has been the sole operating vehicle at the museum, and almost effortlessly it has run day in and day out carrying visitors from the entrance hall to a recreated Black Country village which has been constructed within a canal basin. It is the only narrow gauge car running in Britain, and is a nostalgic reminder of how people in the Black Country travelled to and from work. On its way to the village it passes a colliery typical of the many which once dotted the local landscape. The museum also operates trolleybuses round the grounds and narrow-boat cruises through the Dudley Canal tunnel. Additional trams from various former local systems, such as Dudley and Stourbridge, South Staffordshire, and Wolverhampton, are undergoing restoration.

*Above:* Unique attraction. Douglas horse trams started running in 1876 and are still going strong. Few horse trams exist in the world today - and none can match Douglas for longevity or popularity. All the cars have roller bearings to give a smooth ride and the road surface between the tracks is made of a special bitumen to give the horses a better grip. (Tony Stevenson)

*Right, above:* One in a million! The Black Country Museum's sole operating tramcar, Dudley and Stourbridge No. 5, has carried more than 1,500,000 passengers since 1980.

*Right:* Tickets please! Passengers on the Dudley tramcar receive souvenir tickets.

*Festive occasion! Preserved Blackpool tramcar No. 40 gongs its way through a sea of people at the Fleetwood Transport Festival.*

Black Country Museum

Tipton Road, Dudley, West Midlands DY1 4SQ

**Tel:** 021-557 9643

**Opening times:** Daily (except Christmas Day) 10am-5pm (or dusk if earlier)

**Admission:** Charge payable

**Amenities:** *Free tram rides *Shop *Cafe *Public house *Car parking

**Location:** On A4037, at junction with A4123. Turn off M5 at Junction 2

**Track length:** 600 yards (opened 1980)

**Gauge:** 3ft 6in

**Tramcars:**
DUDLEY & STOURBRIDGE 5
Enclosed 4-wheel single-decker built by Birmingham and Midland Joint Committee 1920

**Undergoing or awaiting restoration:**
DUDLEY & STOURBRIDGE 75
Enclosed 4-wheel single-decker built by Brush 1919

DUDLEY & STOURBRIDGE 23-38 class car
Four-wheel open-topper built by Electric Railway and Tramway Carriage 1901

SOUTH STAFFS 102
Front-exit 4-wheel enclosed single-decker built by Birmingham and Midland Joint Committee 1920

WOLVERHAMPTON 49
Unvestibuled 4-wheel open-topper built by United Electric Car 1909

WOLVERHAMPTON & DISTRICT 34
Enclosed 4-wheel single-decker built by Birmingham and Midland Joint Committee

WOLVERHAMPTON TRAMWAYS COMPANY 23
Double-deck horse tram built by Falcon 1892

# FLEETWOOD

## FLEETWOOD TRANSPORT FESTIVAL

Fleetwood's street transport festival is the only one of its kind in Britain. It is held in July on the town's main shopping thoroughfare, Lord Street, and provides a dazzling display of vintage and veteran road transport vehicles. Historic trams are included in the festivities, and they give rides all day long between Fleetwood Ferry and Ash Street, providing a splendid view of many colourful preserved buses, commercial vehicles, traction engines and other vehicles lining both sides of the route. Street entertainers, fairground organs, a miniature passenger-carrying railway, an exhibition of model trams, and extended licensing hours help make the festival one of Britain's most enjoyable historic transport events.

Fleetwood Transport Festival

Lord Street and Adelaide Street, Fleetwood

*In immaculate condition, this resplendent Glasgow tramcar, known as a Cunarder, is on display at the Glasgow Transport Museum. More than 250 modern trams were built for Glasgow's tramways between 1936 and 1952, and No. 1392, the last of these to be built, saw only 10 years' service before it was put aside for preservation. Between 1962 and 1974 it was exhibited in the Museum of British Transport at Clapham, in South London.*

For further information please contact: Marketing and Promotions Department, Wyre Borough Council, Civic Centre, Breck Road, Poulton-le Fylde, Lancashire FY6 7PU

**Tel:** 0253 891000

**Opening times:** Usually second Sunday in July, 11am-4.30pm

**Admission:** Free, but fares payable on cars

**Amenities:** *Extended licensing hours *Cafes open all day

**Location:** Fleetwood is well sign-posted from M6 via M55 and A585

**Tramcars:** Provided by Blackpool Transport Services subject to availability

## GLASGOW

### GLASGOW MUSEUM OF TRANSPORT

Glasgow has set exciting standards in culture, and a classic example of the improvements in the city's heritage is the Glasgow Museum of Transport. In its new home in the magnificent Kelvin Hall, the museum brings a fresh dimension to static exhibits, with attractive displays which include a reconstructed underground station and a suburban street complete with Regal picture house. There are seven tramcars in the collection, representing Glasgow's renowned tramway system, and they are exhibited on double track, with walkways at upper-deck level so that visitors can peer into the top saloons. A horse tram heads one line of cars, and one of the city's resplendent Cunarder cars the other. Life-size dummies of a conductor and horse tram driver add a touch of realism. Also on display are one of the city's trolleybuses, steam locomotives, and a railway station, motor cars and bicycles, and some 250 models of ships built on the Clyde.

Glasgow Museum of Transport Kelvin Hall, Bunhouse Road, Glasgow G3 8DP

**Tel:** 041-357 3929

**Opening times:** Mon-Sat 10am-5pm; Sun 12-6pm

**Admission:** Free

**Amenities:** *Shop *Cafe *Car parking

**Location:** Opposite Kelvingrove Art Gallery, a mile from city centre on Dumbarton Road

**Tramcars:**

GLASGOW 543
Double-deck horse car built by North Metropolitan 1894

GLASGOW 672
Single-deck 8-wheel 'Room and Kitchen' car built by Glasgow CT 1898

GLASGOW 779
Standard 4-wheel unvestibuled balcony car built by Glasgow CT 1900

GLASGOW 1088
Standard 4-wheel enclosed double-decker built by Glasgow CT 1924

GLASGOW 1089
Experimental high-speed 8-wheel enclosed single-decker built by Glasgow CT 1926

GLASGOW 1173
Streamlined 8-wheel enclosed double-deck 'Coronation' built by Glasgow CT 1938

GLASGOW 1392
Streamlined 8-wheel enclosed double-deck 'Cunarder' built by Glasgow CT 1952
Two tramcar bogies
Various tramway artefacts, and a sculpture of a tramcar winging its way to the great tram shed in the sky.

## GLOUCESTER

### GLOUCESTER TRANSPORT MUSEUM

The Old Fire Station, Bearland, Gloucester

**Tel:** 0452 26467 (Contact curator)

**Opening times:** By appointment only, but exhibits, including horse tram, fire engine and farm wagon, can be viewed through glass doors from street at all times

**Location:** Bearland: from A40 (west) and A38 Bristol road (south)

**Tramcar:**

GLOUCESTER Horse tram (partially restored) built by Starbuck 1880

## GRAMPIAN

### GRAMPIAN TRANSPORT MUSEUM

Alford, Grampian, AB33 8AD

**Tel:** 09755 62292

**Opening times:** Apr-Sep, daily, 10.30am-5pm

**Admission:** Charge payable

**Amenities:** *Shop *Car parking *Play park

**Location:** on A944, west of Aberdeen

**Tramcar:**

ABERDEEN 1
Double-deck horse tram built by Shinnie 1896

## HARTLEPOOL

### GRAY ART GALLERY AND MUSEUM

Clarence Road, Hartlepool, Cleveland TS24 8BT

**Tel:** 0429 266522

**Opening times:** Daily (except Christmas, 1 Jan and Good Friday), 10am-5pm; Sun 3-5pm

**Admission:** Free

**Amenities:** *Shop *Car parking

**Location:** Hartlepool town centre

**Tramway exhibit:**

Electric tramway office of 1900, reconstructed alongside other buildings in museum gardens

A much-travelled tram. Nicknamed 'Kipperbox', this car was built in 1912 for Hull and sold to Leeds in 1942. It was one of the first cars to be acquired by the Tramway Museum Society, operators of the National Tramway Museum, and was preserved successively at Atherton, Bolton and Crich before returning to its native city for display in the Hull Museum of Transport alongside other historic tramcars. (Colin Stringer)

A turn-of-the-century scene at Glasgow Transport Museum. Behind the dummy of a horse tram guard is one of Glasgow's first electric tramcars, No. 672, known as a 'Room and Kitchen' or 'But and Ben' car. The car has rotating destination boards and a centre entrance, with a separate saloon for smokers. After withdrawal from passenger service it became a mains testing car, which ensured its survival until the last days of the Glasgow tramway system.

One of the finest transport museums in Britain is at Glasgow, where the exhibits include two lines of trams headed by this 1894 horse car (complete with dummy crew) and a 1952 Cunarder car. The horse car, which cost £700 when built, took part in the memorable cavalcade which marked the end of Glasgow's famous tramway system on 4 September 1962. Before moving into Kelvin Hall, the museum collection was previously displayed in the former paint shop of the Coplawhill car works, which was converted into museum premises and opened by Queen Elizabeth the Queen Mother on 14 April 1964. The old museum is now 'The Tramway', one of Glasgow's famous theatre venues. Some 20 Glasgow tramcars are preserved in a number of transport museums - all in Britain, apart from one in Paris and one in America.

# HULL

## HULL MUSEUM OF TRANSPORT

Britain's oldest surviving tramcar is preserved in one of the country's oldest transport museums now housed in new purpose-built premises. Dating from 1871, the car is Ryde Pier No 4 (restored as No 3) which is unique in having rounded corners embellished with carvings of grapes. The new museum has imaginative new displays which reveal the story of public transport in Hull through the eyes of its passengers and employees. Visitors can board the trams in the collection (which stand on mixed-gauge track) and listen to tapes evocative of the periods during which they ran. They can also see videos of trams and trolleybuses. Another rare exhibit is an Irish steam tram, and there is a large balcony window which gives a panoramic view of shipping on the River Hull.

Streetlife - Hull Museum of Transport

High Street, Hull HU1 3DX

**Tel:** 0482 222737

**Opening times:** Daily (except Christmas, 1 Jan and Good Friday) Mon-Sat 10am-5pm, Sun 1.30-4.30pm

**Admission:** Free

**Amenities:** *Shop *Limited parking

**Location:** Close to River Hull at Gelder Street end of High Street

**Tramcars:**

HULL 132
Enclosed 4-wheel double-decker built by Hull CT 1909 (On loan from National Tramway Museum)

PORTSTEWART 1
Four-wheel steam tramcar locomotive built by Kitson 1882

RYDE PIER 4
Enclosed single-deck horse car built by Ryde Pier 1871

Model of Hull 101, built for display at British Empire Exhibition 1924

*The oldest tramcar exhibited in Britain is this pier car from Ryde - on display at the Hull Museum of Transport.*

# IPSWICH

## IPSWICH TRANSPORT MUSEUM

The recently-established Ipswich Transport Museum brings together under one roof a collection of 65 vehicles built up since the mid-1960's. It is housed in the former Priory Heath trolleybus depot. The tram body in the collection was used as a shed and summerhouse at Claydon, near Ipswich, for nearly 50 years. It was acquired in 1975 and it is hoped to restore it and eventually to run it on a tramway line, once a permanent site has been found.

Ipswich Transport Museum

Old Bus Depot, Cobham Road, Ipswich

(Correspondence to: 125 Heathlands Park, Ipswich IP4 5TG)

**Opening times:** By arrangement, and on selected dates

**Admission:** Donations appreciated

**Amenities:** *Shop *Limited parking

**Location:** Priory Heath, Ipswich

**Tramcar:**

Undergoing restoration

IPSWICH 33
Four-wheel open-topper built by Brush 1904

# IRONBRIDGE

## BLISTS HILL OPEN AIR MUSEUM

Ironbridge, Telford, Shropshire

**Tel:** 0952 433522/432751

**Opening times:** All year 10am-5pm

**Admission:** Charge payable

**Amenities:** *Shop *Cafes *Car parking

**Location:** On the River Severn in Telford, South of A5. Take Junction 4 from M54 (off M6)

**Exhibit:**

BIRMINGHAM & MIDLAND 12
Body of 4-wheel balcony car built by Brush 1897 (Restored to its latter-day use as a chapel)

# LAUNCESTON

## LAUNCESTON STEAM RAILWAY

Tramway-like carriages hauled by ex-slate quarry steam locomotives make the Launceston Steam Railway an attractive venue for both tramway and railway fanatics. Two of the carriages are based on Manx Electric crossbench trailer cars of 1893. They were built at the railway's Launceston workshop in 1981 and 1988, and carriage No 1 is built on bogies built in America in 1917 for the War Department light railways and used in France during the First World War. The 2ft-gauge railway runs through the beautiful Kensey Valley, where it is possible to catch glimpses of woodpeckers, buzzards, herons, stoats, badgers and other wild life. It is built on part of the trackbed of the old North Cornwall Railwaym and some of the rails were originally used on th Llandudno and Colwyn Bay electric railway. The railway has a rapidly expanding museum of vintage transport and machinery.

Launceston Steam Railway

St Thomas Road, Launceston, Cornwall

**Tel:** 0566 775665

*Trams and steam. Launceston Railway in Cornwall operates carriages based on the design of Manx Electric crossbench trailers (Hugh Ballantyne)*

**Opening times:** Daily, Whit-Sep; Sun and Tues only, Easter to Whit and October; also weekend afternoons in Dec (Santa Specials) and Easter weekend

**Charges:** Tickets are valid for unlimited rides on day of issue

**Amenities:** *Shop *Two cafes *Car parking

**Location:** Near town centre, on B3254 road to Bude

**Route length:** 2 miles (Opened 1983)

**Gauge:** 2ft

**Rolling stock:**

No 1 Manx Electric type crossbench carriage 1981

No 2 Manx Electric type crossbench carriage 1988

No 67 Four-wheel glazed saloon, 1983

Ex-Inny Valley Railway bogie car, 1980

# LIVERPOOL

## LIVERPOOL MUSEUM

(Part of National Museums and Galleries on Merseyside)

William Brown Street, Liverpool L3 8EN

**Tel:** 051-207 0001

**Opening times:** Daily (except Christmas, New Year and Good Friday) Mon-Sat, 10am-5pm; Sun 12-5pm

**Admission:** Free

**Amenities:** *Shop *Cafe

**Location:** In city centre, a few minutes' walk from Lime Street Station

**Exhibits:**

Liverpool Overhead Railway coach No 3 built by Brown, Marshall 1892

The National Museums and Galleries on Merseyside also own LIVERPOOL 245, a streamlined 4-wheel enclosed double-decker built by Liverpool CT 1938, which at time of going to press was in storage and not on view to public.

*This single-deck Amsterdam car, the only Dutch tram running in England, started life as a trailer in 1929, but was motorised in 1938. It was donated in 1980 to the East Anglia Transport Museum, where it now runs with trolley pole instead of bow collector. The museum, which contains a varied collection of vehicles, was founded on its present site in Chapel Road, Carlton Colville , in 1965, and was opened to the public in 1972. (Alan Lindley)*

*A tram ride through a scenic wood is one of the enjoyable attractions offered by the East Anglia Transport Museum at Carlton Colville, near Lowestoft. After the closure of London's tramways in 1952, this car, No. 1858, spent some years at Chessington Zoo in Surrey before being moved to Lowestoft. Built for the London County Council in 1930, mainly for use on hilly routes, it is now the mainstay of the museum's operating fleet.*

# LLANDUDNO

## GREAT ORME TRAMWAY

Mountains in England, Ireland, Wales and the Isle of Man can be seen from the summit of the Great Orme cable tramway, which rises 679ft above sea level. The cars are hauled by cable, and passengers have to change cars at Halfway Station. The average gradient on the lower half of the line is 1 in 6.5 and on the upper half 1 in 15.5. The cars run in competition with a cabin lift between the summit and Happy Valley.

Great Orme Tramway

Victoria Station, Church Walks, Llandudno

**Tel:** 0492 870870

**Opening times:** Daily from Good Fri to 1st week Oct, 10am-5.45pm

**Charges:** Fares payable

**Amenities:** *Shop *Car parking on street or in York Road car park

**Location:** Close to town centre

**Track length:** 1 mile (opened 1902)

**Gauge:** 3ft 6in (Maximum gradient 1 in 3.9)

**Rolling stock:**

Nos 4-7 Enclosed 8-wheel single-deckers built by Hurst Nelson 1902/3

*Victoria cable car station at Llandudno, with car No. 5 in new livery waiting to climb the Great Orme. (Stuart Rivers)*

*Four London electric tramcars are displayed in the London Transport Museum, housed in the old Covent Garden fruit market, including this West Ham car, No 102. (Ian Dougill)*

# LONDON

## LONDON TRANSPORT MUSEUM

London Transport Museum provides a stimulating and educational outing for those who want to discover more about the history of London Transport. The collection of historic vehicles is displayed under one roof - in the former flower market of the rejuvenated Covent Garden. Trams, buses, trolleybuses and trains are well represented. They include the luxurious and progressive Feltham type tramcar (with extended driver's cab), which was introduced by the Metropolitan Electric Tramways in 1931 to combat the growing competition from buses and private cars.

*Glasgow standard car No. 585, sole tramcar on display in the Science Museum, arrives there on 11 November 1963, after stopping near Hyde Park Corner to observe the two-minute silence.*

London Transport Museum
39 Wellington Street, Covent Garden, London WC2E 7BB

**Tel:** 071-379 6344 (24-hour recorded information 071-836 8557)

**Opening times:** Every day (except 24-26 Dec) 10am-6pm

**Admission:** Charge payable

**Amenities:** *Shop

**Location:** Close to Covent Garden underground station

**Tramcars:**

LCC 1025
Enclosed 8-wheel double-decker built by LCC 1908

LONDON TRAMWAYS 284
Double-deck horse tram built by John Stephenson of New York 1881 (Withdrawn for restoration)

METROPOLITAN ELECTRIC 335
Enclosed 8-wheel double-decker built by Union Construction 1931

WEST HAM 102
Four-wheel unvestibuled balcony car built by United Electric Car 1910

## SCIENCE MUSEUM

Exhibition Road, South Kensington, London SW7 2DD

**Tel:** 071-938 8000

**Opening times:** Daily (except Christmas), Mon-Sat, 10am-6pm; Sun, 11am-6pm

**Admission:** Charge payable

**Amenities:** *Shop *Cafe

**Location:** Nearest underground station - South Kensington

**Tramcars:**

GLASGOW 585
Four-wheel standard enclosed double-decker built by Glasgow CT 1901

BOURNEMOUTH 85
Eight-wheel open-topper built by United Electric Car (On loan to Bournemouth Transport Museum)

CHESTERFIELD 8
Single-deck horse tram built by Milnes 1899 (On loan to National Tramway Museum)

DOUGLAS 14
Double-deck horse car built by Midland Railway Carriage and Wagon 1883 (On loan to Manx Museum, Douglas)

DOUGLAS HEAD 1
Four-wheel crossbench open-topper built by Brush 1896 (On loan to National Tramway Museum)

GATESHEAD 10
Eight-wheel enclosed single-decker built by Gateshead and District Tramways 1925 (On loan to Beamish Museum)

SHEFFIELD 264
Four-wheel double-deck balcony car built by United Electric Car 1927 (On loan to Beamish)

(See also Swindon for Science Museum Wroughton)

# LOWESTOFT

## EAST ANGLIA TRANSPORT MUSEUM

Trams and trolleybuses run side by side at the East Anglia Transport Museum, which has one of the most varied collections of preserved commercial vehicles in Britain. Set on the outskirts of Lowestoft, close to Oulton Broad, this museum both delights and surprises its visitors. For it encapsulates in a timeless way the fascination of yesteryear's urban transport scene - bringing back memories of more leisurely and civilised times before the days of supermarkets, graffiti, inflation and mini-buses. The entire project has been developed by a small dedicated voluntary group of transport lovers, with little outside help or financial assistance. The trams, which give rides through a stretch of woodland, include a single-deck car from Amsterdam. Buses, trolleybuses, motorcars, taxis and other commercial vehicles are all well represented, the trolleybuses alone numbering more than a dozen.
A period street, complete with authentic furniture, is being developed. There is also a narrow-gauge railway.

East Anglia Transport Museum
Chapel Road, Carlton Colville,
Lowestoft NR33 8BL

**Tel:** 0502 518459

**Opening times:** Easter-Sep, Sun
and Bank Holidays, from 11am;
June-Sep, Sat, from 2pm; August,
Mon-Fri, from 2pm

**Admission:** Charge payable

**Amenities:** *Free vehicle rides
*Shop *Cafe *Car parking (enter
via Hedley House Hotel)

**Location:** 3 miles south west of
Lowestoft on B1384

**Track:** 500m (opened 1972)

**Gauge:** Standard

**Tramcars:**

AMSTERDAM 474
Four-wheel saloon single-decker
built by Beijnes 1929

BLACKPOOL 11
Enclosed 8-wheel 'Vambac'
single-decker built by English
Electric 1939

BLACKPOOL 159
Enclosed 8-wheel double-decker
built by Blackpool CT 1927

GLASGOW 1245
Enclosed 8-wheel Coronation
double-decker built by Glasgow
CT 1939

LONDON 1858
Enclosed 8-wheel HR2 class
double-decker built by English
Electric 1930

LOWESTOFT 14
Four-wheel open-topper built by
Milnes 1904

**Awaiting restoration:**

LCC trailer car (1915)

LOWESTOFT eight-wheel
combination single-decker

NORWICH 39, a four-wheel
open-topper built by English
Electric 1924

*Granada Television's replica tramcar No. 21 takes visitors to Coronation Street.*

# MANCHESTER

### GRANADA STUDIOS TOUR

Checkpoint Charlie may no
longer exist in the real world
- but a replica of it is included
in the Granada Studios Tour,
making it the only place where
unsuspecting tram passengers
can come face to face with
East German border guards.
The trams, too, are make-
believe.  They are rubber-
wheeled trackless replicas of
the vehicles that once ran

*Snacks from a mock tram on the Granada Studios Tour*

*Parkland pleasure riding in Manchester! Heaton Park's electric tramway, now extended to the boating pool landing stage, gives Manchester a unique attraction which parks in London and other English cities are unable to rival. The section of track on which the trams are running was originally part of the tramway sidings laid in the park by Manchester Corporation Tramways in 1905. An elaborate large tram shelter, constructed in 1906 to accommodate a large number of waiting passengers, now serves as a depot for the park's trams. The tramcars are manned and maintained entirely by volunteers.*

in many cities. The tram tour also takes visitors to two streets well-known to TV viewers - Coronation Street and Baker Street. And hamburgers can be bought from a tram used as a snack bar.

Granada Studios Tour

Water Street, Manchester, M60 9EA

**Tel:** 061-833 0880

**Opening times:** Tues-Sun, Summer, and Wed-Sun, Winter

**Admission:** Charge payable

**Amenities:** *Shops *Cafes and restaurants *Car parking

**Location:** In Castlefields area of city

**Rolling stock:**

Six replica trams:- two 4-wheel open-toppers (Nos 20 & 50), three 4-wheel short-roof open-toppers (Nos 21-23), and a single-decker used as a snack bar

## HEATON PARK VINTAGE TRAMWAY

Many a romance blossomed on the upper deck of trams running out to city parks. Today, the romance of the tram can be savoured in the attractive setting of Heaton Park in Manchester. Enthusiasts have uncovered derelict tram track, originally laid in the park grounds in 1905, and now operate trams through the park - one of the largest in Britain - from the Middleton Road entrance to the main boating lake. One of

*Passengers aboard Manx Electric car No. 19 enjoy this view of Douglas Bay from Howstrake cliffs as they head for Douglas. (Isle of Man Transport)*

*The world's longest-running tram, Manx Electric car No 1, at the delightful tree-lined Laxey station, also the departure point for Snaefell cars. (Tony Stevenson)*

the three cars operated on the tramway is a restored survivor of the city's famous 53 circular route, which was operated until its closure in 1930 by single-deck 'combination' cars.

Heaton Park Vintage Tramway Middleton Road, Manchester

**Tel:** 061-682 0652 or 061-432 2789

**Opening times:** Good Friday to Mid-Oct, Sun and Bank Holidays, 12-5pm; July to Mid-Aug, Wed, 10.30am-3pm

**Charges:** Fares payable on cars

**Amenities:** *Shop *Car parking

**Location:** On A576, near end of M66.

**Track:** 745m (opened 1979)

**Gauge:** Standard

**Tramcars:**

BLACKPOOL 600 (ex-225) Open 8-wheel single-deck 'boat' built by Blackpool CT 1934 (On loan from Blackpool Transport )

HULL 96 Enclosed 4-wheel cut-down double-decker built by Hurst Nelson 1901

MANCHESTER 765 'California' type 8-wheel single-decker built by Manchester CT 1914 (On loan from National Tramway Museum)

Also display of artefacts

## MANCHESTER MUSEUM OF TRANSPORT

Boyle Street, Cheetham, Manchester M8 8UL

**Tel:** 061-205 2122

**Opening times:** Wed, Sat, Sun and Bank Holidays, 10am-5pm

**Admission:** Charge payable

**Amenities:** *Shop *Cafe open Sundays only *On street car parking

**Location:** At rear of Queen's Road bus depot

**Tramcar:**

Undergoing restoration

SOUTH LANCS 65 Unvestibuled 4-wheel balcony car built by United Electric Car in 1906

# MANX COAST

### MANX ELECTRIC RAILWAY

The world's longest-running electric tramcars are still at work on the Isle of Man - carrying passengers on the Manx Electric Railway. Nearly 100 years old, cars 1 and 2 were built in 1893 for the opening of the line, and are mentioned in the Guinness Book of Records. All the Manx Electric cars (apart from fire replacements) are more than 80 years old. They run 18 miles between Douglas and Ramsey, offering some splendid views of mountains, glens and coastline, and giving an ever-changing vista unrivalled by any other seaside line in the world today. The most spectacular view on the line is at Bulgham, where the cars run along the top of cliffs 600ft above the sea. The railway sells Rover tickets, which allow passengers to break their journeys to explore some of the glens en route, like that at Groudle where there is a mile-long miniature passenger-carrying railway.

Manx Electric Railway

Department of Tourism and Transport, 1 Strathallan Crescent, Douglas, Isle of Man

**Tel:** 0624 663366

**Opening times:** Easter-Sep, daily; Oct-Apr, Mon-Fri

**Charges:** Fares payable on cars or at Douglas, Laxey and Ramsey stations

**Location:** In Douglas the terminus is at Derby Castle (end of horse tramway) and in Ramsey it is on Parsonage Road, off Albert Street

**Route length:** 18 miles

**Gauge:** 3ft

**Rolling stock:**

24 motored 8-wheel single-deckers and 24 trailers as follows:

Nos 1-2, 5-7, 9, 19-22 (motored saloons); 14-18, 25-33 (motored crossbench cars); 57-59 (enclosed trailers); 36-37, 40-51, 53-56, 60-62 (crossbench trailers).

All were built 1893-1906 by Milnes, except 28-33, 55-58 and 61-62, which were built at Preston 1904-6, and 40, 41 and 44, built as fire replacements 1930 by English Electric (Car 22 was fire-damaged 1990).

# MILTON KEYNES

## MUSEUM OF INDUSTRY AND RURAL LIFE

Stacey Hill Farm, Southern Way, Wolverton, Milton Keynes MK12 5EJ

**Tel:** 0908 316222/319448

**Opening times:** May-Oct, Wed-Sun, 1.30-4.30pm

**Admission:** Charge payable

**Amenities:** *Shop *Car parking

**Location:** At north end of city, off H2, Millers Way

**Exhibits:**

Section of the original steam tram track laid out in setts

Awaiting restoration

Parts of two WOLVERTON & STONY STRATFORD steam tram trailers built by Midland Railway and Tramway Carriage in 1887

# OAKHAM

## RUTLAND RAILWAY MUSEUM

Ashwell Road, Cottesmore, Nr Oakham, Leics LE15 TBX

**Tel:** 0780 63092/62384

**Opening Times:** Weekends

**Admission:** Charge payable on steam days; otherwise free, but donations requested

**Amenities:** *Shop *Refreshments *Car parking *Picnic areas

*Exhibits at the St. Helens Transport Museum include this Blackpool tramcar, No. 641, built in Coronation year. (St. Helens Transport Museum)*

**Tramcar:**

WISBECH & UPWELL 7
Steam tramway coach awaiting restoration

# RAMSEY

## MANX ELECTRIC RAILWAY MUSEUM

MER Station, Ramsey, Isle of Man

**Opening times:** May to Sep, Mon-Fri, 11am-4pm

**Admission:** Donations box

**Amenities:** *Shop *Adjacent car parking

**Location:** At terminus of Manx Electric Railway

**Tramcars:**

DOUGLAS 11
Horse-drawn toastrack built by Starbuck 1886

DOUGLAS 47
Horse-drawn roofed toastrack built by Milnes Voss 1911

DOUGLAS 49
Horse-drawn convertible car built by Vulcan 1935

MANX ELECTRIC 26
Eight-wheel single-deck goods

car, formerly passenger car 10 built by Milnes 1895

RAMSEY PIER
Petrol locomotive and passenger trailer built by Planet in 1937

Also steeple-cab electric locomotive and displays of photographs, posters and other items, including overhead equipment, compressor controller, Snaefell roof board, and two Mather & Platt electric motors.

# ST HELENS

## ST. HELENS TRANSPORT MUSEUM

An historic tram and bus depot which successively housed horse, steam and electric trams, trolleybuses and buses, is now the home of the St Helens Transport Museum. The museum, which is run by the North West Transport Museum Society, has nearly 100 vehicles in its collection, including two tramcars. One of the trams is a Coronation class tramcar from Blackpool, originally acquired by the Coronation Tramcar Preservation Society. The depot still contains tram track and remnants of the trolleybus overhead wiring system.

St Helens Transport Museum

Old Bus Depot, 51 Hall Street, St Helens WA10 1DU

**Opening times:** Easter-end of Sep, Sat and Sun 12-4pm

**Admission:** Charge payable

**Amenities:** *Shop

**Location:** Close to centre

**Tramcars:**

BLACKPOOL 304
Enclosed 8-wheel Coronation single-decker built by Charles Roberts 1952

Awaiting restoration:
WARRINGTON 2
Enclosed 4-wheel double-decker built by Milnes 1902

*Above:* A novel experience in tram travel - riding the narrow-gauge line at Seaton in Devon. These two cars, Nos 8 and 12, have been operating at Seaton since the line opened in 1971. (Seaton and District Electric Tramway Co.)

*Right:* This car, No. 02, now serving as a shop at the Seaton terminus, started life as a well-equipped construction car.

## SEATON AND DISTRICT ELECTRIC TRAMWAY

Bird watchers have a field day when they ride on the Seaton narrow-gauge tramway on the south coast. For it runs alongside the scenic Axe estuary affording close-up views of more than 50 species of birds, including kingfishers, herons, cormorants, Canada geese and oyster catchers. The narrow-gauge Edwardian-style trams are popular with holidaymakers, and give a six-mile round trip between Seaton and Colyton. The tramway follows the route of the former Seaton Junction branch line of the London and South Western railway, felled by the Beeching axe in 1966. Some of the track was laid with second-hand rail acquired from the Sierra Leone railway, and some of the overhead equipment came from Hamburg.

Seaton and District Electric Tramway

Harbour Road, Seaton, Devon EX12 2NQ

**Tel:** 0297 21702

**Opening times:** Easter to end Sep, daily; October only, Mon-Fri; Nov-April, limited winter service

*Some you can buy, some you can't. Shipley Glen tramway's shop is a museum as well as a retail outlet.*

*A ride up the Shipley Glen tramway puts day trippers on the road to the moors. This car, in 1895 livery, is at the Top station*

**Charges:** Fares payable

**Amenities:** *Mobile tram shop at Seaton *Shop and cafe at Colyton

**Location:** Off A3052 and B3172. Follow signs for Seaton or Colyton

**Track length:** 3 miles (Opened 1971)

**Gauge:** 2ft 9in

**Rolling stock:**

No 2 Open-topper, 1961; No 4 Open single-deck boat, 1961; No 6 Open-topper, 1956; No 7 Open-topper, 1958; No 8 Open-topper, 1968; No 12 Open-topper, 1961 (rebuilt 1979); No 14 Enclosed single-decker, 1984; No 17 Crossbench single-decker, 1988.

All the cars are 8-wheelers and were built by Seaton Tramways and its predecessor, Eastbourne Tramway Company (Modern Electric Tramways Ltd)

# SHANES CASTLE

### SHANES CASTLE RAILWAY

The atmosphere of the old Irish roadside light railway has been recreated on Shanes Castle railway near Antrim. The track runs through the castle's nature reserve along the edge of Lough Neagh, and the rolling stock includes three tramcars from Charleroi in Belgium, which are used as trailers, mainly in wet weather. Shanes Castle is the family seat of the O'Neills of Clanaboy and commands views over the length and breadth of the Lough.

Shanes Castle Railway
Shanes Castle, Antrim, Northern Ireland BT41 4NE
**Tel:** 084 94 28216

**Opening times:** Suns, Apr to Mid-Sep; Sats, Jul-Aug; Weds, Jun-Aug, plus Easter (except Good Fri), Bank Hols and certain July days

**Admission:** Charge payable

**Amenities:** *Shop *Cafe *Car parking

**Location:** One mile from Antrim, on A6 Antrim-Randalstown road

**Track length:** 1.5 miles (opened 1971)

**Gauge:** 3ft (914mm)

**Rolling stock:**

CHARLEROI 38, 41 & 42 Enclosed 4-wheel trailers

# SHEFFIELD

### SHEFFIELD BUS MUSEUM

Tinsley Tram Sheds. Sheffield Road, Tinsley, Sheffield S9 2FY
**Tel:** 0742 553010

**Opening times:** Easter-Dec, open days held on certain days, 12-4pm; also every Sat and Sun when members working on exhibits

**Admission:** Charge payable

**Amenities:** *Shop *Limited car parking

**Location:** On A6178, close to Meadowhall Shopping Centre. Take Junction 34 off M1

**Tramcar:**

Undergoing restoration
SHEFFIELD 460
Four-wheel enclosed double-decker built by Cravens 1926

# SHIPLEY

### SHIPLEY GLEN CABLE TRAMWAY

Bradford trolleybus enthusiasts run the Shipley Glen tramway, a narrow-gauge cable-hauled line which gives a ride through a bluebell wood up the side of a steep hill. Attractions at the top of the tramway include a fairground, countryside centre, glen cafe and public house. At the bottom, a short walk takes visitors to the Victorian village of Saltaire, with its mill, church and almshouses.

Shipley Glen Cable Tramway
Prod Lane, Shipley, West Yorkshire BD17 5BN
**Tel:** 0274 589010

**Opening times:** Easter-Oct, Sat 1-5pm, Sun and Bank Hols, 10am-6pm; also Wed from June-July, 10am-4pm. Santa Specials, December

**Charges:** Fares payable (at either top or bottom stations)

**Amenities:** *Shop *Car parking

**Location:** Off A6083, near junction with A657

**Track length:** 386 yards (opened 1895)

**Gauge:** 1ft 8in (Maximum gradient 1 in 12)

**Rolling stock:**

Four toastrack single-deckers, coupled in pairs, built by Webbs Trucks 1956

# SNAEFELL ISLE OF MAN

### SNAEFELL MOUNTAIN RAILWAY

On a clear day you can see England, Scotland, Ireland and Wales from the summit of Snaefell in the Isle of Man. The summit can be reached by riding on electric cars of the Snaefell Mountain Railway, which climb 2036ft in half an hour, giving a panoramic view of the whole island en route. On the way up, the cars pass Lady Isabella, the island's famous water-wheel, and at Bungalow they cross the world-renowned TT motor-cycle race course. They climb the mountain on the right-hand track and descend on the left-hand track, both tracks being fitted with the Fell braking rail to prevent derailments.

*Birkenhead Tramways No. 7, restored by the British Horse Tram Enthusiasts, is the oldest preserved double-deck horse car in Britain. It was built in 1876. (RS Jones)*

the Pwllheli Corporation and Pwllheli and Llanbedrog lines. Following its withdrawal from service in 1927, it served as a chicken coop, and from 1969 until 1986 was successively an information kiosk and waiting room outside Pwllheli railway station. Steam locomotives and carriages, railway artefacts, steam rollers and vintage buses, are also on display at the Centre, which is housed in a former railway terminal.

Southport Railway Centre
Derby Road, Southport,
Merseyside PR9 OTY

**Tel:** 0704 530693

**Opening times:** 11am-5pm weekends May-Sep; 1-5pm daily June and 1st week Sep and weekends Oct-Apr; 10.30am-4.30pm daily July-Aug. Special events and steam days throughout the year; Santa Specials December

**Admission:** Charge payable

**Amenities:** *Shop *Light refreshments *Parking

**Location:** Few minutes' walk from town centre via London Street

**Tramcars:**

BIRKENHEAD TRAMWAYS 7
Double-deck horse car built by Starbuck 1876

PWLLHELI 4
Single-deck 3ft-gauge horse car built by Falcon 1897

---

Snaefell Mountain Railway
Strathallan Crescent, Douglas, Isle of Man

**Tel:** 0624 663366

**Opening times:** May-Sep, daily

**Location:** Cars start from Laxey Station, served by Manx Electric cars from Douglas and Ramsey

**Charges:** Tickets purchased from Douglas, Laxey, Ramsey, Bungalow or Summit stations

**Amenities:** *Shop and cafe at Summit

**Route length:** 4.75 miles

**Gauge:** 3ft 6in (average gradient 1 in 12)

**Rolling stock:**

Nos 1-6 Enclosed 8-wheel single-deckers built by Milnes 1896

## SOUTHEND

### PIER MUSEUM

Southend Pier Museum Foundation, 36 Shaftesbury Avenue, Thorpe Bay, Essex

**Tel:** 0702 614553

**Opening times:** May-Oct, Fri-Mon 11am-6pm

**Admission:** Charge payable

**Location:** Beneath North Station of Pier. Access from Pier Station

**Exhibits:**

Southend Pier cars Nos 22, 2 and 11 built by AC Cars 1949

1929 Signal box

To be restored;

Original 1890 toastrack

## SOUTHPORT

### SOUTHPORT RAILWAY CENTRE

Southport Railway Centre boasts the oldest preserved double-deck street horse tramcar in Britain. It is Birkenhead 7, built in 1873, which was acquired for preservation in 1972 from a Southport coal merchant and is now being restored by the British Horse Tram Enthusiasts. The Enthusiasts are also restoring Pwllheli single-deck horse tram No 4 at the Railway Centre. It is believed this car ran on both

*Looking resplendent after countless hours of restoration, Swansea tram No. 14 combines the lower deck of one car with the upper deck of another. It is a lowbridge car built by Brush in 1924, and its design is based on the low-height cars evolved at Cardiff. Twenty-seven trams like this were built for operation in Swansea, where the operation of double-deck trams had hitherto been limited because of the many low bridges in the town. They had a seating capacity of 64, excellent riding qualities and were economical to operate It is proposed to eventually operate Swansea 14 on a short tramway. (Swansea Maritime and Industrial Museum)*

*Snaefell car No. 4 picks up passengers at Laxey Station before climbing to Snaefell Summit 2036ft above sea level. (Isle of Man Transport)*

# SWANSEA

## MARITIME AND INDUSTRIAL MUSEUM

Tramway exhibits at this museum include a Swansea city tramcar, No 14, which has been restored after serving for 40 years as a farm building at Ammanford. The truck used in its restoration is from a Brussels 4000 class single-decker. There are also two exhibits from the Swansea and Mumbles electric line, the last tramway to close in Wales. The museum plans to build a quayside tramway.

Maritime and Industrial Museum Museum Square, Maritime Quarter, Swansea SA1 1SN

**Tel:** 0792 650351

**Opening times:** Daily, 10.30am-5.15pm (except Christmas Day, Boxing Day and 1 Jan)

**Admission:** *Free

**Amenities:** *Shop

**Location:** In maritime quarter

**Tramcars:**

SWANSEA IMPROVEMENTS 14 Four-wheel low-height enclosed double-decker built by Brush 1924

SWANSEA AND MUMBLES 2 Front cab of electric car built by Brush 1924

SWANSEA AND MUMBLES Replica of double-deck horse car

Birdwatchers once used this Stockport tram as a hide - on Matley Moor at Rowarth, near Stockport. Since 1972, however, it has been undergoing restoration and reconstruction (for most of the time by one man working alone), and it is planned to run it on one of the country's heritage tramways. The car ran in Stockport for nearly 50 years, for the last 32 years of its life as a balcony car. Most of the reconstruction was carried out at the Southport Railway Centre. A support group for the car was formed in June 1991, but the car is not yet on show to the public. (British Aerospace)

# SWINDON

## SCIENCE MUSEUM WROUGHTON

Red Barn Gate, Wroughton, Nr Swindon, Wilts SN4 9NS

**Tel:** 0793 814466

**Opening times:** May-Sep, selected weekends, 10am-5.30pm

**Admission:** charge payable

**Amenities:** *Shop *Refreshments *Car parking

**Location:** On A4361

**Exhibit:**

SOUTH STAFFS
Four-wheel tramcar truck built by Leeds Forge 1892

# WALSALL

## WALSALL STEAM RAILWAY

Arboretum Park, Walsall,

**Tel:** Walsall 30078 or 22544

**Opening times:** Every Sun, Summer and Winter 2-6pm

**Location:** On Broadway North, signposted from A34, M5 and M6

**Track length:** Approximately half a mile of double track

**Gauge:** Seven and a quarter inch

**Tramcars:**

No 8 Birmingham enclosed double-decker (1981)

No 9 Swansea and Mumbles double-decker (1984)

Nos 10 & 12 Birmingham rapid transit cars (1984 and 1988)

# SOME OTHER PRESERVED TRAMCARS

The following cars are awaiting or undergoing restoration or are in store awaiting permanent display in a museum or on a line planned for construction:

**BIRKENHEAD 20**
Four-wheel open-topper built by Milnes 1900, undergoing restoration at Birkenhead

**BLACKPOOL 298**
Eight-wheel single-deck railcoach built by Brush 1937, undergoing restoration in the Greater Manchester area

**BRIGHTON 53**
Four-wheel open-topper built by Brighton CT in 1937, awaiting restoration in Brighton area

*Rapid transit cars have reached Walsall - in miniature form. This car, No. 10, runs at the Arboretum Park. (Richard Wall)*

**BRUSSELS 5016**
Eight-wheel single-decker built at Charleroi 1935, in store at Leadon Valley, near Gloucester, for eventual operation on proposed tramway between Ledbury and Gloucester

**CHELTENHAM 21**
Four-wheel open-topper built by English Electric 1921. (Negotiations are under way to transfer this car from Bournemouth to Cheltenham Art Gallery and Museums, who hope to eventually restore it and put it on display as part of an enlarged Cheltenham history gallery.)

**CRUDEN BAY 1 or 2**
Four-wheel single-decker built by Great North of Scotland Railway 1899, undergoing restoration by Aberdeen City Arts Department

**DUNDEE & DISTRICT 2 and 23**
Steam tram trailers built by Starbuck (1882) and Milnes (1895) undergoing restoration at Birkenhead

**EDINBURGH 226**
Four-wheel double-decker built by Dick, Kerr 1903 undergoing restoration at Lothian RT central garage, Edinburgh (Visits by prior arrangement; ring 031-447 4334)

**EXETER 19**
Four-wheel open-topper built by Dick, Kerr 1906 awaiting restoration at West of England Transport Collection, Winkleigh, Devon

**FALKIRK 14**
Eight-wheel single-decker built by Brush 1931, restored at Falkirk Museums' Workshops in Grangemouth for eventual operation on a line in Callender Park, Falkirk

**GLASGOW 1016 and 1017**
Four-wheel single-deckers built for Paisley by British Electric Car in 1904, undergoing restoration by the Scottish International Tramway Association and Summerlee Transport Group

**HUDDERSFIELD 31/39**
Four-wheel open-topper built by British Electric Car 1902, awaiting restoration at Acre Mill, Golcar (Visits by prior arrangement, ring 0484 654133)

**KREFELD 41 and 412**
Single-deckers built by Duwag 1956/7 in store at Abbey Park Road bus depot, Leicester. (Appointment to view necessary).

**LIVERPOOL 762**
Eight-wheel enclosed double-decker built by Liverpool CT 1931, under restoration in Birkenhead

**LUTON 6**
Four-wheel balcony car built by United Electric Car 1908, being restored by Luton Museums at Stockwood Park

**MANCHESTER L53**
Double-deck horse tram, under restoration at Horwich, Bolton

**MANCHESTER 173**
Four-wheel open-topper built by Brush 1901, undergoing restoration at Horwich, Bolton

**MANCHESTER, BURY, ROCHDALE AND OLDHAM 84**
Four-wheel steam tram locomotive built by Beyer Peacock 1886 awaiting restoration in store at the Manchester Museum of Science and Industry

**MODERN ELECTRIC TRAMWAYS 23**
Miniature 15-inch gauge enclosed centre-entrance tramcar in store at Birkenhead

**NEATH GAS TRAM**
Built 1896 by Ashbury and restored by Neath BC Training Agency at Millands Road, Neath

**NORTHAMPTON 21**
Four-wheel open-topper built by Dick, Kerr 1905, awaiting restoration in Conwy Valley, North Wales

**NOTTINGHAM 101**
Four-wheel balcony car built by Dick, Kerr 1901, awaiting restoration at Wymeswold, Leics

**NOTTINGHAM 45 and 92**
Four-wheel balcony cars built by Dick, Kerr 1901/2, awaiting restoration in Nottingham

**OXFORD**
Remains of horse trams Nos 6, 20, and ex-NorthMet 707 at Oxford Bus Museum.

**PORTSDOWN AND HORNDEAN 5 and 13**
Four-wheel open-toppers built by British Electric Car 1903, awaiting restoration in Old Portsmouth

**PORTSMOUTH 84**
Four-wheel open-topper built by Milnes 1891 in store at Portsmouth

**RAWTENSTALL 23**
Four-wheel single-decker built by United Electric Car 1911, awaiting restoration in the Greater Manchester area

**SOUTHAMPTON 11**
Four-wheel domed-roof double-decker built by Southampton CT 1923, undergoing restoration in Southampton for City Museums

**SOUTHAMPTON 38**
Four-wheel open-topper built by Hurst Nelson 1903 undergoing restoration in Southampton

**SOUTHEND PIER 7 and 21**
Four-wheel enclosed single-deck rail coaches built by AC Cars 1949, in store in the Conwy Valley, North Wales

**STOCKPORT 5**
Four-wheel open-topper built by Dick, Kerr 1901, undergoing restoration in Greater Manchester area

**SWINDON 13**
Four-wheel open-topper built by Brush 1920, acquired for restoration by Leadon Valley Electric Railway Association for its proposed tramway between Ledbury and Gloucester

**WALLASEY 78**
Four-wheel short-roof balcony car built by Brush 1920, undergoing restoration in Birkenhead

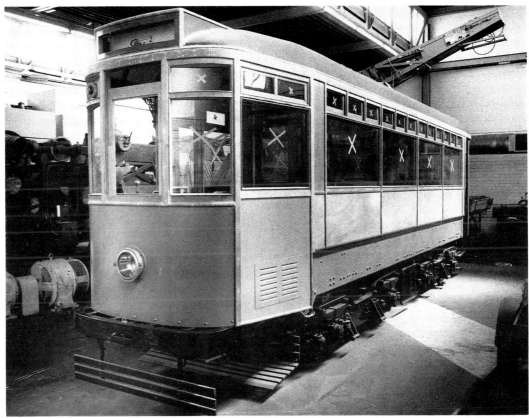

*Restoration of Falkirk tramcar No. 14 nears completion by Falkirk Museums. This car was one of a fleet of pullman cars introduced on Falkirk tramways in 1929-31. It could reach 35mph and had transverse one- and-two seating. (Falkirk Museums)*

*Brussels 5016 in store (Leadon Valley Electric Railway Association)*

# TRAMWAY RELICS

Tramway relics, such as shelters, track, overhead poles and depots survive or are preserved in a number of towns, reminding us of the part tramcars played in our transport heritage.
In Huddersfield, for instance, an old steam tram shelter at Edgerton is still used by bus passengers. Other surviving shelters, erected for electric trams, include three in Brighton, two in Darwen, two in Hyde, Cheshire, and one near the South Pier in Lowestoft.

In a number of towns, sections of tram track have been preserved or are still lying where they were left when tram operation ceased. The following are some of the places where tram track can be viewed:

BARROW - Ramsden Dock Road
BIRMINGHAM - Edmund Street
DARWEN - Whitehall
DUNDEE - Murraygate
EDINBURGH - Waterloo Place
HUDDERSFIELD - Bus station
LONDON - Southampton Row
PORTSMOUTH - Rugby Road
ROCHDALE - Yorkshire Street
SHEFFIELD - The Moor

*More than a century old, this steam tram shelter at Edgerton in Huddersfield is still in use - as a bus shelter*

*A monument to the tramway era. These novel tree holders, standing on preserved track, remind Sheffield shoppers that The Moor shopping precinct was once a major tram thoroughfare.*